ONE FOOT IN THE WATER

By Steve Charles

May THE LIGHT shine on ALL the creatures of the Universe

A magical journey of the mind which makes an impassioned plea on behalf of animals.

This book will appeal to animal lovers, the kind-hearted, the open-minded and those with an interest in the realms of mind, body and spirit.

It takes the reader on a journey through the lives of various animals subjected to man's cruelty, and, while at times it may sadden you, its central character, Nirvana, the Divine Dolphin, will also bring great comfort and hope to those sensitive humans who truly care about the welfare of their animal friends.

Although written in a light, lively style, the book has a powerful and profound message.

If it touches your soul, please tell others.

Animals, just like humans, need and deserve our compassion!

COPYRIGHT

DEDICATION

I dedicate this book to all the beautiful and precious pets who have shared a part of my life.

FOREWORD

Hello there. I've been waiting for you to find me. I've been so looking forward to meeting you.

My name is Steve and you and I were destined to meet. You have been guided here so that I can tell you about the most incredible, wondrous journey I have just returned from.

To say it was the trip of a lifetime would be an understatement. Some would say it was out of this world.... and you will see what they mean.

I've told some of my friends already. Some laughed sarcastically, while others were literally swept off their feet and have taken the first steps on their own voyage of enlightenment.

Anyway, you have always been noted for your open-mindedness, so read on and judge for yourself. You could be in for a mind-blowing experience!

THE JOURNEY

My journey began one morning when I woke up feeling a bit out of sorts. There was no particular reason. Some mornings I bounced out of bed and felt on top of the world. Other days I wished I was marooned on a desert island, isolated from civilisation and all it entailed.

A girlfriend used to attribute my contrasting mood patterns to my Gemini birth sign, saying I was a classic example of a split personality.

She used to say that on a good day even if I broke both legs I would still have a joyful smile for everyone. By contrast, on a bad day, she would say that even if I won a million pounds on the lottery, I would still look as if I had all the cares of the world on my shoulders.

Anyway, this was definitely one of the latter days. There was no known cure for my "down" days, but I decided that a change of scenery might lighten the gloom.

I got in my car and headed for the coast, about an hour's drive away. It might have been mid-October, cold and overcast, but I had an irresistible urge to head for the sea.

I turned on the radio. The Beatles' record, Here Comes The Sun, a favourite of mine, was playing. For once, I turned it off. I just wasn't in the mood.

When I reached the coast, I was not surprised to find the beach empty. It was drizzling and there was a light mist.

Nevertheless, I wandered across to the pebbly beach and crunched my way down to the water's edge.

Visibility was poor, but I could see a large rock a little way from the shore, perched upon which was a single seagull.

I bade him good day and moved on. I had been walking a few minutes, enjoying the soothing sounds of the waves as they broke and gently rolled across what little sand this beach boasted, when I suddenly heard my name being called.

I stopped dead in my tracks, surprised I was no longer alone. I looked around to see who was calling, but could see no-one within my admittedly limited vision.

"Hello," I stuttered. I heard the voice call again: "Stephen". Although I could see no-one, I did not feel uneasy. It was such a soft, kind, gentle voice.

I am very sensitive to the tone of voices and I instinctively knew this belonged to someone I would like.

I called out: "Hello, who is there? Please reveal yourself." A few seconds passed without a reply when, for a third time, I heard my name.

This time, however, I was told where to look for my mystery companion.

"Stephen, I am behind you," came the sweet, sensual and slightly mischievous voice again.

I swivelled round and looked out to sea, feeling slightly silly as no-one in their right mind would be swimming in the chilly autumn sea.

But there was no mistaking where the voice had come from. I stared blankly out to sea when, suddenly, a great whoosh of water exploded in front of me, followed by a great, grey shape leaping up out of the water. I watched it rise and then somersault before nosediving back into the sea.

I stepped back in wonderment. Seconds later, the most beautiful creature I had ever seen lifted its head out of the water.

I tell you, I have never seen a face like it. It was the cutest, friendliest and most joyful face imaginable. This hypnotic creature took my breath away.

It spoke. "Hello Stephen. My name is Nirvana and I am a dolphin. Well, more accurately, I am your spiritual feminine... your guiding light... pleased to meet you at last."

"Where did you come from, you gorgeous creature?" I heard myself say, still mesmerised by the beauty of this divine dolphin.

"Oh, I've been alongside you all your life, hitching a ride," laughed Nirvana. "I was just waiting for the right time to introduce myself."

"Nirvana, you are so incredibly beautiful," I gushed like some love-struck teenager. "Your face... it glows with love and joy. Just looking at you makes me feel so happy.

"I had been feeling sorry for myself, but right now I feel truly uplifted, all thanks to seeing you."

"Glad to be of assistance," smiled Nirvana.

"You have a pretty name, too", I added. "What does Nirvana mean?"

"It means LAND OF LOVE," replied Nirvana, and as she said it I swear I felt a shiver run down the entire length of my spine, followed by a sensation for which I cannot find adequate words.

The best description I can manage is to say it felt like what some people tell you heaven is like.

"Nirvana, I want to go to the land of love. Take me with you," I begged.

Nirvana laughed. "It is not a place," she said. "It is a state of mind. However, it is attainable if you are prepared to undertake a very special kind of journey."

"Tell me more," I pleaded.

"If you are prepared to search day and night, never wavering from your course despite many temptations, while demonstrating the three key virtues LOVE, WISDOM AND COURAGE, then you can reach Nirvana in this lifetime.

"But I must warn you - you will have to resist fierce opposition, ridicule and hurt."

"I am ready to start my journey," I assured Nirvana. "I know nothing can deflect me from my course."

Nirvana laughed infectiously and then commanded: "Look down at your feet."

I peered down just as a wave swept towards me. It encircled one of my feet, but expired just short of my other foot, which remained dry.

"Look," said Nirvana. "You already have one foot in the water. Looks like your journey has begun!"

I wondered what sort of a trip lay before me and what I was supposed to do now, when Nirvana told me: "Look, I will give you a little push-start, but soon you will be your own guide. You will know instinctively what to do.

"Now, listen very carefully and then do as I say," she instructed, knowing full well I would follow her every command.

"Move up to the top of the beach, lie down and make yourself comfortable. Then let the gentle sound of the waves wash through you until you are perfectly relaxed.

"Then," said Nirvana, "picture my face in your mind's eye and know that I am there to protect you. Finally, start to repeat softly to yourself the magic word: OM.

"Keep saying it over and over, gently and quite slowly:

"OMmmm, OMmmm, OMmmm, OMmmm, OMmmm, OMmmm..."

I was hopelessly under Nirvana's bewitching spell. I ran to the top of the beach. I lay down and listened to the waves lapping the shore. When I felt relaxed, I visualised Nirvana's radiant, glowing face with that dazzling smile that said simply: "I LOVE YOU".

I immediately felt in perfect harmony with the world, engulfed by incredible peace. I started to repeat the word OM. I said it gently, to the rhythm of my breathing.

I cannot tell you how long I lay there. Time seemed to lose all sense of meaning. I had entered a state of peace that was beyond time as we know it.

Suddenly, something amazing happened. My body shook from head to toe and then my world went purple......

All I could see was purple light everywhere. No shapes, no objects, just a glorious blaze of purple as far as I could see.

Was this heaven? I wondered. But before I had time to decide, the purple haze lifted and I found myself standing in my own back garden - next to my favourite apple tree.

I moved closer and peered down on to a large leaf and saw a ladybird and a spider perched side by side *

Now, I've always been a bit fearful of spiders like so many people. But for some reason I felt not a trace of fear now... in fact, I bent down to stroke both insects.

The ladybird seemed to enjoy my tender touch, but as my finger descended towards the spider, he shot out of sight and hid somewhere in the dense undergrowth of leaves.

I felt incredibly sad that I might have frightened the timid creature and pleaded with it to come out so that I could apologise.

To my astonishment, the spider answered me, in a nervous, shaky voice.

"No, go away you bully," said the spider. "I haven't done you any harm, why do you wish to kill me? I suppose it is because I haven't got a nice, shiny red body like the ladybird and don't move in a graceful fashion."

I felt incredibly upset that the spider thought I would hurt him.

"Kill you? I could never kill you," I tried to re-assure him. "I think you are beautiful and I want us to be friends.

"I don't judge by appearances, but by actions. The colour of your skin is irrelevant."

The spider spoke again. "I can't believe you. I know humans don't like spiders. Only the other day, my brother suffered a horrible, torturous death when a human poured scalding hot water over him. You think we are ugly and want to destroy us."

"Well, I don't," I protested. "I used to, but for some reason I feel nothing but the deepest love for you. I can't understand why you don't believe me."

"I tell you something," replied the spider. "If you were me, then you would understand how I feel... only too well."

Just then, something incredible happened. I felt my body shudder and my head started spinning. When it ceased, I felt different.

Suddenly, it dawned on me - I had turned into the spider. I was no longer a strapping, six-foot male human being, but a quivering, timid spider.

I was sitting in a beautiful web I had spun in a hedgerow. It was a bright, summer's day and I was sitting there minding my own business, drinking in the warm sunshine, when I saw a group of schoolchildren approaching.

As they drew near, one of the girls saw me and shrieked. Honestly, you would have thought I had leapt out and attacked her.

"Eeeugh!" she shrieked. "An ugly, creepy, disgusting spider." All the girls in the group started screaming hysterically.

Gosh!, I thought, I must be so grotesquely ugly. I felt unloved and began to cry. I tried to slink away so that nobody would have to look at me, but one of the boys had crept up and he threw out his hand.

Before I had time to make a move, he clenched his fist tight and I was trapped.

It was dark and frightening. I was in danger of being squashed and I was trembling.

I wondered what was going to happen to me and I started to cry again. What was it, I wondered, that had caused them to treat me in this way?

I could hear the other boys moving closer and then I saw daylight again as my prison gates opened. I looked up at six pairs of dark, glaring eyes.

I was shaking with fright. One of the boys grabbed one of my legs. "Owwwwwwwwwwwwwwwwwwww," I cried.

I screamed out in terror and then unbearable pain as my leg was ripped from my body. I was sobbing uncontrollably.

But my ordeal was far from over. Another boy grabbed another of my legs and, as I screamed out in pain, he pulled it clean away from my body.

A third leg was grabbed and then yanked free, much to the amusement of the schoolchildren.

Any hope I might have had of escaping my torturers had gone. I didn't have the legs to carry me and my pain was so terrible, I wished I could be put out of my agony.

But I was still alive and I could not imagine worse suffering.

The boy in whose hand I was stranded cried out: "Yuk, there is all gooey fluid oozing out of the spider's body onto my hand. Messy creature!"

He dropped me and I thudded to the ground. I prepared for a long, lingering, painful death. But one lad raised a foot and mercifully squashed me into the ground.

Instead of pain, I felt a surge of light flash through me. Then I started to rise along a long silver cord. Up and up I went until I reached a brilliant white light soaring high in space.

As I merged with the white light, I felt a serene peace. In this state of tranquil bliss, I looked down on planet earth.

After some time, I felt compelled to descend back down the long, winding silver cord which still connected me to the earth.

When I reached the base of the silver cord, I was able to gaze down on the spot where I had spent my last moments as a spider.

There was my old spider's body, now unrecognisable as a dark brown stain on the pavement. It drew no shrieks of panic from passers-by. They didn't even notice it.

I remembered the schoolchildren, who had caused me such pain and terror. I felt no hate towards them. I just felt sadness and sorrow that they had valued my life so cheaply, if indeed they understood that I had had a life at all.

Just then, I heard a familiar voice. It was Nirvana the dolphin.

"How are you finding your journey?" she asked. "Are you enjoying it? Or have you had enough? You can turn back at any time you like, you know."

"Nirvana, why did you do that to me?" I demanded. "I trusted you. Why did you put me through such pain?"

"Me?" exclaimed Nirvana. "I didn't make you do anything. You chose to experience those events through your own free will.

"I can't make you do anything. You make your own decisions. Just like it will be your decision now - whether to continue on your journey, or turn back.

"Please remember, Stephen, I have no power over you. The only power is WITHIN you."

I could feel the love in Nirvana's voice and suddenly her breathtakingly beautiful face appeared before me.

I was ready to trust her again. Okay, so strictly speaking, I was my own master. But who was she kidding?

I was hopelessly under her potent spell. There wasn't a seductress in the world to match her.

"Send me on my way again," I sighed. "Good boy," she smiled, her eyes twinkling sensuously. "Don't forget, this is your choice......"

Nirvana's face disappeared from view and as it did so, my world once again turned purple.

The warm purple haze lingered for some time before slowly evaporating. As it cleared, I found myself in a beautiful, unspoilt forest.

Majestic, proud trees towered towards the skies. Pretty waterfalls cascaded into fast-flowing rivers and streams, while the clean, fresh air was alive with magical sounds.

Insects were buzzing, birds sang their love songs and monkeys swished noisily from branch to branch.

The world truly is at peace with itself here, I thought.

I heard a rustle in the long grass in front of me and stepped back. Through a small gap, I spied a magnificent, muscular tiger.

Although I knew tigers were powerful lords of the jungle, capable of killing with one leap and grasp of their powerful jaws, I felt no fear.

But as I moved closer, I sensed fear in the tiger. He started to shake with fright.

The tiger cowered and started to back away from me, all the while keeping his nervous eyes fixed on me.

"Don't go beautiful tiger," I urged. "Please stay here with me, let us be friends."

The tiger continued to slink away, but blurted out: "You must be mad if you think I am going to stick around and let you shoot me dead, or worse still skin me alive."

I was hurt. "How could you think I am capable of such a wicked deed?" I protested.

The tiger replied. "What do you expect me to think? My experience tells me that humans hate tigers and will inflict terrible cruelty on us.

"Humans murdered my girlfriend last week. They shot her in front of my eyes. The sound of her groaning as she drew her final breaths is a memory that haunts me day after day, night after night."

The tiger was crying uncontrollably. I wanted to go and hug him and apologise for my fellow humans' unforgivable and despicable actions, but knew he would have every right to attack me.

"If you were me," he sobbed, "you would understand why I feel so threatened when I see humans."

I wanted to fling my arms round the heartbroken tiger, but before I could move, I felt a familiar shiver down my back.

I felt light-headed for a while. When the sensation subsided, I felt different altogether......

I turned my head and looked back at my long, sleek body. I had beautiful markings, bold orange and black stripes. I was a proud and masterful tiger, king of the jungle I surveyed.

I stretched lazily and then started to pad off towards the shade of some nearby trees.

As I did so, the ground beneath my front paws gave way. I toppled forwards and felt myself tumble head over heels into a large pit.

My ankles felt broken and I had no chance of springing free of my prison. I was trapped.

Soon, I heard human voices approaching. They advanced until they were at the edge of the pit.

A man cried out in celebratory fashion when he saw me cowering in the corner of the pit.

"We've got one, we've got one," he shouted back to his comrades triumphantly.

"A fine figure of a beast he is, too," he gloated, "with a magnificent glossy coat. Should be worth a pretty sum."

His fellow-poachers had joined him. One man pointed a rifle at me. He fired and a long dart flashed out and landed in my backside.

It stung for a while, but then I began to feel drowsy as a tranquilising drug was released into my bloodstream.

When I awoke, I found both sets of my paws tied together. The men were in the pit with me. One was brandishing a glowing, red-hot poker. He held it aloft as another man grabbed my tail and lifted it.

The first man thrust the steaming poker through my anal cavity until it ran the length of my belly - leaving my precious coat unblemished.

"AAAAAAAAAAAARRRRRRRRRRRGGGGGGGGGG GGGHHHHHHHHHHHH!"

My screams must have been heard for miles around, but death was swift.

I felt myself rise serenely along a long silver cord until I reached a pulsating white light, where I felt indescribable peace and calm.

Despite its beauty, after some time, I knew it was time to drift down the silver cord descended beneath me.

When I reached the bottom, I found myself looking down on my once-proud tiger's body. Now bereft of its fur, it comprised a sorry heap of bones and flabby flesh.

Vultures were circling expectantly overhead, eager to feast on my carcass.

Nearby, I saw the hunters laying my skin out on the ground and measuring its length.

They were congratulating themselves on their bravado. I felt no animosity towards them. Just pity at their mindless, callous brutality and total absence of sensitivity.

I had seen enough, and, as if on cue, the purple haze descended upon me, blotting out all around.

After a while, it began to clear and I found myself hovering over a grand-looking building in the middle of a busy city.

I lowered myself through the roof of the building as if it didn't exist. I was now in a large ballroom full of self-important looking people in expensive-looking clothes.

I felt strangely magnetised to a group of people with loud, booming - and to my mind immature - voices near the centre of the room and to one woman in particular.

I floated over and realised why I had been so powerfully drawn to this woman.

She was wearing a tigerskin coat. I looked closely - it was my old tiger's coat; there was no mistaking those markings. Great sadness welled up inside me.

"Love the coat darling," drooled one of her companions, "You look simply divine."

"No she doesn't," I shouted, "She looks hideous, grotesque." I was crying, but no-one heard me.

Still I shouted, hysterically, "That's my coat, not hers. Imagine if I killed you, stole your skin and said it belonged to me."

No-one shared my outrage. The woman continued to draw admiring comments wherever she went in the room of ignorance.

I had seen and heard enough. The topics of conversation seemed inane, cold and plastic. Each person seemed to be feeding another's ego.

One brash, flash man was telling another woman whose face was caked with paint how he had a personal fleet of seven super-powered cars - one for each day of the week.

Then he bragged: "Each one has a tiger in its tank."

I felt sick.

Suddenly, I felt myself move away from this room full of verbal pollution. As I did so, the warm purple haze descended upon me.

I felt calm and peaceful again. Through the purple haze, I felt the presence of Nirvana, even though I could neither see nor hear her.

I visualised her irresistible, comforting smile and, as if by magic, she entered my world again.

"Still here?" she asked unnecessarily. "Isn't it all getting a bit much for you? Don't you want to go back to your safe old world and pretend all this suffering never existed?" she asked.

"Nirvana," I said, "I have experienced pain and suffering, sorrow and sadness. But it was the spider and the tiger who really experienced it. I realise it is going on all the time and yet previously I have turned a blind eye.

"But look Nirvana, as well as drawing love and compassion from you, you also seem to fill me with courage. Please give me the strength to see this through to the death."

For the first time there was a hint of disappointment in Nirvana's voice. "Haven't you learnt yet that there is no such thing as death?" she asked. "Just interludes between lifetimes.

"And another thing. Why do you ask me to give you strength? Remember what I said - the power is WITHIN you, you just have to learn how to unlock it.

"There is certainly nothing to fear, Stephen. For you are immortal. Everyone is."

I gulped as I tried to digest what Nirvana was stating. Then she spoke again.

"You have come a long way along the path that leads to the LAND OF LOVE - but there is still a considerable way to go. And always remember - fear is the obstacle to love."

Nirvana disappeared and I was all alone again. I sighed, and as I did so, the purple haze started to clear.

In its place was a bright, glistening white carpet of snow, stretched as far as I could see.

It was the coldest place on earth. But I felt completely at home.

I glanced down at my feet. Four of them. Creamy white in colour. I was a polar bear and I loved this place.

It was my kingdom. I loved to run and frolic in the unspoilt, expansive freedom of the Arctic. I could think of no greater joy than rolling about playfully in the ice and diving into the clear blue sea to splash about.

I looked behind me, and there were three innocent bundles of creamy-white fur. I was a doting mother polar bear.

I fell on to my side and the cubs each fought for a nipple and started to suckle eagerly. I felt deep contentment. I had everything I could possibly wish for.

After my babes had finished their feed and fallen asleep, I crept off to find some food to keep my strength up.

I had gone a little way when I saw a ship chugging along in the not-too-far distance. Then, another whirring-type noise started up and a strange-looking object rose from the ship into the sky.

I watched intently as the flying object - which I later heard described as a helicopter - started to move towards me.

Instinct told me it was time to get back to my babies.

I ran as fast as my legs would carry me, but the helicopter was faster. I tried to step up the pace, but I was struggling for breath and the machine in the sky was now directly overhead.

As I looked up, I could see it was bearing down on me. I saw a door at the side open and a man lean out and hurl a large blackish object out.

As it fell, it spread out into a massive net. It dropped on top of me, blurring my vision and bringing me to a virtual standstill.

The helicopter landed and several men jumped out and stood round the edges of the outstretched net, pinning it to the crisp snow. I was trapped.

I was very frightened and my heart was pounding. One man wielded a rifle and took a pot shot at me. I felt a dart shoot into my rear. I felt brief pain... and then lost consciousness.

When I awoke, I was in unfamiliar surroundings. Gone was the glistening thick carpet of snow I so loved.

I was now in a soulless, concrete prison in an establishment known by humans as a zoo.

Four walls surrounded me. The floor was bare except for a small pool of water, barely big enough for me to turn round in.

I looked up above the high walls and saw some people peering down at me.

"Oh, look mum, isn't it lovely?" I heard a little girl coo. "I think it's my favourite animal in the whole zoo."

"Yes, darling. Polar bears come from the coldest regions of the world," said her mother, matter-of-factly.

I tried to call up to her: "Yes, that's right. So what am I doing here in this concrete prison, miles from my beloved homeland?"

"And if I am so nice, why has your species stolen me, separated me from my family and deprived me of my freedom? Please tell me what crime I committed."

I wanted to confront the woman and her husband and demand of them: "How would you like it if I broke into your house in the middle of the night, kidnapped your daughter and took her back with me to the polar regions and stuck her in a tiny cage for all my friends to come and gawp at?"

I just wanted them to think. To forget about themselves for just a little while and consider whether they had the right to subject me and the other creatures in the zoo to our awful misery.

I began to think of my own little infants back home.

I wondered what fate had befallen them. Had they starved to death? Or, even worse, had they been found by my captors and were now in alien surroundings, frightened to death?

I couldn't bear to think about it. I began to cry out loud and my head felt like it was going to explode.

No-one seemed to notice my anguish. I could hear the crowds above. I heard them describe me as cute, loveable and cuddly. I am afraid these were not descriptions I could apply to them.

A little door opened at the back of my prison and a hand appeared and tossed some dead fish into the small pool.

I had to jump into the pool to satisfy my hunger, but more importantly, it seemed, to provide some entertainment for the hordes. A notice above the wall read: 'Polar bears fed at 3pm'.

I dived in dutifully and devoured the fish. The crowd were delighted and cheered and clapped.

Was I supposed to bow?

I wished the ground would open up and swallow me.

I wandered endlessly, day after day, up and down my cramped cell. My fur had lost its shine and I had a constant migraine. I had lost the will to live - but had no means to put an end to my misery.

One evening, after the zoo gates had been closed to the public, the man who tossed the fish into the pool each day at 3pm, arrived at my cell, along with the manager of the zoo.

They seemed uncharacteristically concerned about my welfare.

"What's wrong with Snowy, then Joe?" asked the zoo manager.

"I'm afraid the poor creature's in a bad way, guv'nor," said Joe. "She just seems to sway her head from side to side all day long and her eyes seem to have a sinister stare these days.

"I don't know for sure boss, but I think she's gone mad."

"I see, Joe," said the manager. "But do you think the public have noticed?"

"Well," said Joe. "Most don't seem bothered. But some of the regulars have commented to me that Snowy doesn't seem her usual self these days."

"In that case, she'll have to go," said the manager without emotion. "There's plenty more where she came from. They're not on the endangered list yet."

The manager looked Joe in the eyes and said simply: "You know what to do..."

They were right of course - I had gone mad. And if the public cottoned on it could affect the click of the turnstiles and, well, their wages had to be paid.

I was at my lowest ebb. I had not a friend in the world. Every second of every day was a nightmare. I curled up in the corner of my cell and cried myself to sleep.

I was awoken some time later by the clink of the door at the back of my cage. Joe's hand poked through and tossed me a fish. I noticed a bright orange capsule sticking out of its side.

I ate the fish and started to lost consciousness as Joe's final words echoed through me: "So long old girl, it's been a pleasure knowing you."

I felt myself float up along a long silver cord towards a radiant white light. I became part of the white light and rested in its incredible warmth and peace.

After some time, I felt compelled to descend again along the long silver cord.

When I reached the bottom, I slipped into a bright purple haze. Through the mist I saw Nirvana's ever-welcoming face.

"Oh, Nirvana," I cried. "I have never been so pleased to see you.

"I must tell you everything. It was terrible, just terrible. I was a polar bear that went mad after a life of incredible cruelty and torture."

Nirvana pointed out: "There are lots of polar bears and other creatures throughout the world suffering similar and far worse fates. You haven't seen anything yet."

"Why? Why? Why?, Nirvana," I shouted. "Why do we allow it to happen?"

"Because," said Nirvana, "not enough people are looking for the LAND OF LOVE. They are too pre-occupied with the land of SELF, which manifests in the form of material possessions, wealth for wealth's sake or meaningless titles to place before or after a person's name."

She added: "It is a choice they make and one for which they will be accountable at the end of a lifetime.

"It is a choice you can make still Stephen. Do you want to turn a blind eye to all you have seen so far? I shan't complain."

"I shall see this thing through to the end," I vowed. "I must experience it all, no matter how much pain is entailed. Others may choose short-term gain, but I shall journey on until I reach the LAND OF LOVE.

"You told me I am immortal - and I believe you Nirvana."

She looked at me with what looked like pride in her eyes and then started to fade from view - as I knew she must.

After she had gone, the purple haze began to lift. In its place was a vibrant, lush forest.

I looked down from a great height and realised I was in a tree. I was singing. Singing for joy.

I looked alongside me and saw a beautiful, brightly-coloured parrot and some newly-born parrot chicks. I was one of the clutch of baby parrots.

I couldn't have felt happier and I chirped long and loud, sharing my joy with all the inhabitants of the forest.

After a while, I began to feel hungry and I could hear my brothers and sisters' stomachs rumbling, too.

Mum sensed our hunger. She kissed each of us in turn and then flew off to find us some food.

Shortly after she had left, I felt the tree shaking. Perhaps it was a monkey climbing the tree. I waited for the disturbance to pass.

Then I became aware of human voices, and as I peered over the top of our nest to see what was happening, my world went pitch black.

It had been a human intruder climbing our tree and he had smothered me with a cloth and was holding it so tight, I struggled to breathe. Eventually, I passed out.

When I awoke from my slumber, I found myself in a tiny cage in a town house. The magical sounds of the forest had gone, replaced by a deathly silence.

I turned round and saw a big, hefty man built like one of the gorillas who inhabited our forest, standing peering in at me.

He moved even closer and I noticed words tattooed on his chunky forearms. One declared: HATE; the other EVIL.

"Right parrot," he boomed. "My name is Butch and yours is Polly."

He added in his gruff voice: "I've bought you to impress the birds. Not your sort of bird - but my sort. Those delightful creatures shaped like this."

His hands outlined a curvy shape as a horrible, sickly grin spread across his face.

"If I can teach you to say some witty phrases, they are bound to be impressed," he said.

I felt an affinity with these other type of "birds". He clearly had equal disdain for us both.

He was now right up against my cage. I noticed a smell on his breath.... a smell I was to come to know well - and fear. It was, I learnt, caused by something called alcohol.

For days he tried to get me to repeat such enlightened phrases as: "Butch is brave... Butch is strong... Butch is sexy".

Brave? Strong? Sexy? Who was he kidding? To me he was a sad, pathetic, pitiful creature.

I could have repeated his words. But I was not going to be bullied into anything, especially not for someone who had robbed me of my liberty and the love of my family and sentenced me to a hell-like existence in a tiny, cramped cage.

Day by day, I sensed Butch getting angrier as I refused to mimic his mindless phrases.

Eventually, he started using scare tactics. He would get into a terrible rage and start banging my cage.

When that didn't work, he tried blackmail, leaving me without food and water.

The final straw came one night when he arrived home stinking of alcohol. I had been deprived of food and water for three days. The once-beautiful plumes of my wings had nearly all fallen out. I knew I looked a feeble, pathetic creature - a description I had always applied to Butch.

My life was a terrible prison sentence and I wished I could hang myself.

I no longer dreamed of soaring through the clear blue skies of my tropical paradise. Swooping to glide on the breeze was an experience - normally a parrot's birthright - which I was never to know.

I might as well have been born without wings.

Anyway, this particular night, Butch came over and started banging furiously on my cage.

"Women," he boomed, as if I was keen to hear his words of wisdom, "they're all the same. Lead you on, take your money and then show you the door."

I maintained my silence, quaking inside. Then he informed me: "And you are no better. Call yourself a parrot? You are supposed to be clever and able to talk.

"But just take a look at yourself. A feeble bag of bones, with the intelligence of a paper bag."

He banged on the cage again and I trembled with fear. He flung open the door and made a grab for me. I bit him as hard as I could.

He screamed out in agony. "Why you little bastard," he hollered, managing to grab me round the neck.

I screeched and then he tightened his grip until I could hardly breathe.

"You are a waste of space," he bellowed. I managed a muffled scream. "Oh, you have finally found your voice have you?" he mocked. "Well you're just a little too late....."

He drew back his arm, took aim and hurled me with great force at the far wall.

I desperately tried to flap my wings, but they failed to respond... and I smashed head-first into the wall. I felt nothing.....

I was attached to a long silver cord that soared high into the sky and beyond. I rose along it until I melted into a dazzling white light.

I sensed Nirvana's presence. "My God, Nirvana," I sighed.

"An interesting choice of words," she teased.

"That was as bad an experience as I have gone through yet," I told her. "Torture of the most appalling kind."

Nirvana had now revealed her physical self and I basked in her tender, loving aura.

'Incredibly, I feel compelled to go back for more," I assured her. "Apart from which, I'm frightened that if I turn back, you will disappear from my life. And that is something I just cannot contemplate."

"Bon voyage," whispered Nirvana. "See you again on your next stopover." She faded from view.

I waited for the purple haze - and sure enough it was soon engulfing me.

When it cleared again, I felt immensely strong and empowered.

As my eyes regained full vision, I found myself staring into a large lake.

I looked around and saw some deer drinking from it, while a couple of spider monkeys played chase near the water's edge.

I peered down into the water and saw reflected back at me a truly magnificent figure of a big bull elephant, with huge gleaming tusks.

I was that elephant. And even if I say so myself, a mighty handsome beast I was. Behind me were my family; my wife and young son.

I decided to take them both for a stroll through the bush. We were ambling along, minding our own business, when I heard a motor vehicle approaching.

That's funny, I thought. I haven't seen any tourists around here for a while.

I guessed they would want me to pose for some photographs as usual and, as I had nothing pressing to worry about, I waited for them to approach.

A Jeep drew up to within a few yards and a couple of big chaps jumped out.

I puffed out my chest in my favourite pose and waited for the click of their cameras.

But when I looked down at the object being pointed at me, I got a surprise. It was a long and pointed shape - and definitely not a camera.

I stepped forward to get a better look. But as I did so, an explosion rang out and a searing pain shot through my chest.

I trumpeted out in pain and agony. The animals of the bush screamed out at the thunderous force of it. Trees shook as if an earth tremor had hit the region.

I felt my legs collapsing and I fell ungracefully into a writhing heap. Blood gushed from my chest with the force of a burst water main.

I groaned long and loud as I lay in a reservoir of my own blood.

My final sight before my heart managed its last beat was of my young son bawling his eyes out and my wife screaming hysterically.

We elephants have photographic memories. This was a scene my family would remember for the rest of their lives, each gory, graphic detail.

I drifted up along a long silver cord towards a breathtaking white light. I stayed and rested in its tranquillity.

But soon I felt it was time to move down the silver cord again. I began my descent and soon found myself hovering above my discarded elephant's carcass.

I saw my tormentors. Without a flicker of emotion, one of them was knelt over sawing away eagerly at one of my tusks.

He continued sawing until the tusk came away from my former head. He then turned his attention to the second tusk, while a companion started polishing the severed one.

Strangely, I felt no bitterness, no anger. Incredibly, I felt great waves of compassion for these cold-blooded mercenaries.

They showed no remorse for taking another creature's life in exchange for monetary gain. But I was able to forgive.

After all, they had once been born into the world as innocent, divine creatures.

It was their tragedy that somewhere along the road of life they had been ambushed and seduced by ego-related temptations and SOLD THEIR SOULS.

I wondered what was to become of my old tusks. A sudden "flash" of insight told me that they would be sculpted into such "beautiful" creations as ear or neck adornments for humans or else into delicate, intricate ornamental pieces to grace sideboards or mantelpieces.

I had seen enough.

I visualised the warmth of the purple haze, and as if by magic it descended upon me.

Seconds later, there was my darling Nirvana. I awaited her words of wisdom, but was surprised to hear her offer praise.

"I congratulate you on your courage, Stephen," she said. "You have been prepared to experience first-hand the suffering of others - and have not flinched from the course I set before you.

"You truly laid aside your SELF to enter the world of others."

"I know one thing, Nirvana," I whispered. "My life will never be the same. How could it be? But tell me Nirvana, did all those experiences happen in the real world or were they a mystical vision I chose in order to see a less personalised view of the world?"

"Save your questions for just a little longer, Stephen," said Nirvana. "Your journey has not quite reached its conclusion. Be prepared for a spectacular finale. Just one more experience...."

Nirvana faded into the purple haze, which itself started to rise and evaporate.

I pushed down with my feet, but failed to ground myself. I just seemed to bob up and down. I felt buoyant.

I looked around me and found myself miles out at sea.

I reached down with my arms and felt my legs submerged in the water. I felt my thighs, my knees and my toes. These were human legs all right. I had not incarnated as a different species this time.

I was human Steve and I was drifting miles out to sea without another soul in sight. This was a real test. Was I frightened now? I had been told I was immortal and that no harm could come to me.

But what if everything had been an incredible dream? What if I had just fallen asleep on the beach that misty morning and the incoming tide had swept me out to sea?

I dipped my head in the water to try and clear my mind and as I did so, I saw alongside me the most awesome dark shape. It seemed to stretch for ever.

It was right alongside me. I stretched my arm out and pushed on it to lever myself away.

But as I touched it, it purred with delight. I felt its ecstasy run through my arm and then throughout my entire body.

Instead of moving away, I edged closer and started to run my hand gently, sensuously along its huge body as if caressing the woman of my dreams.

This incredible creature enjoyed my tender touch. The gentle vibrations of its purring swept through me.

I felt great love for this immensely powerful but gentle creature. I stretched my arms lovingly around her and wished I could merge with her.

As I looked down at her, I was amazed to find I was looking at her with x-ray vision. As I peered into the vast cavern of her body, all I could see was a sea of pink. It looked heavenly.

Suddenly, I was sucked inside... and enveloped in sheer, pink LOVE. I truly felt I had entered heaven.

This was a place where only love existed. I wished everyone could feel it. I wanted to share this sublime, heavenly land of love with everyone. Nothing could remotely compare with it.

I never wanted to leave, but this wondrous creature started to move and I realised she had her own journey to make.

I felt immense gratitude that she had allowed me to know her so intimately, to feel her warmth and love.

However, I didn't own her and reluctantly I swam out of the mass of pure pink bliss and floated up to the surface of the sea.

I saw a large ship heading towards me. I realised I had to get back to land some time and I started to wave to the crew.

The ship drew closer and I noticed a harpoon-like object at the front of the deck. A man shouted down to me: "Get out of the way, you silly young fool. Unless you want to be killed along with the whale."

A spear-shaped object shot from the front of the ship. Travelling at lightning speed, it flew past me and pounded into the body of my beautiful friend, the whale.

She let out the most pitiful, haunting sound I have ever heard as blood spurted from her body high into the air, like a volcano erupting.

My heart felt as if it was exploding in sympathy. I started to shake uncontrollably and I began to vomit.

The sea all around me was a thick, treacly red, with my sick floating on top.

I looked up at the boat. Were these really my fellow human beings I saw up there raising their hands in triumph, gloating with self-satisfaction?

I cried out, my voice breaking up. "You are evil. Why have you killed my friend? My beautiful, kind, gentle, loving friend. She never hurt anyone in her life."

In fact, my whale friend was not quite dead. She let out one more horrible, piercing scream - the most dreadful cry of anguish imaginable.

I started to swim towards her. "Don't die, don't die my baby, please don't die," I begged her.

She spoke.

"I don't blame you. I know you love me," she said, "I just want to know why they wanted my blood. I wished no-one any harm.

"But you must not grieve for me oh sensitive one. You have been told you are immortal. Well, so am I, I have to shed this body now, but I shall return one day. Goodbye for now. I love you."

I lay sobbing at the senseless, wicked murder of this sacred creature.

I prayed for the purple haze to return and help me erase this gruesome, heart-wrenching memory.

But this time it didn't come.

Surely Nirvana hadn't deserted me now. I had trusted her with my life..... correction with my various lives.

Tears were cascading down my cheeks like mini waterfalls. I watched them being swallowed up by the sea, when suddenly I thought I heard Nirvana's voice. But this was not her usual warm, happy greeting.

She was wailing. Horribly. Sorrowfully. She was clearly in great distress and I had to get to her to try and save her.

"Nirvana," I screamed. "Where are you? What's wrong? I'll save you my precious sweetheart."

I sensed the direction of her whimpering and began swimming frantically.

"God, give me strength," I requested. "Take my life and save Nirvana's."

I felt an incredible bolt of strength surge through my entire body.

I swam with renewed vigour, until finally I could make out Nirvana's body through the murky water.

I stopped sharply in my tracks as I caught sight of Nirvana's face.

It was horribly different. The ever-present smile had gone. Sure, her lips were still shaped in an upward curve. But she looked sad, gaunt, listless. Her eyes no longer glowed, but looked heavy and pained.

She looked at me, but didn't have the strength to grace me with her usual loving welcome. Her body no longer glistened with radiance, but was dull and weak.

It seemed to have a criss-cross pattern running over it. As I moved in closer, I realised it was not part of her body, but that it was a fisherman's net she had become entangled in.

She had obviously been fishing for her dinner and got trapped in the net.

What angered me was that the fishermen above must have heard her distress, but done nothing to free her.

I tugged feverishly at the rope entwined around her feeble and rapidly-weakening body.

She had been trying to liberate me from the ego-centred world, but now her own struggle for freedom threatened to kill her. She was weakening by the second.

I looked down at her sad, soulful eyes and prayed: "God, give me strength."

I felt another charge of strength shudder through my entire body.

I tugged furiously at the net. I felt a snap and Nirvana managed to wriggle free.

We rose to the surface in unison.

I remembered what she had told me, that she was not really a dolphin, but a manifestation of my spiritual feminine being... my guiding light.

The beautiful Beatles song, Something, a real favourite of mine, started playing in my head.

I stretched my arms tenderly around her, bowed my head, and, lost to the world for I couldn't tell you how long, I covered her with soft, delicate, sensitive licks and kisses.

She was vibrating.

Suddenly, she trembled, gasped loudly, and then whispered dreamily and sweetly into my ear: "A giver not a taker, I see. How very appropriate. I should have known. Now you have transported me to another world... sensitive...... sublime....... heavenly.... thank you!"

I was in another universe.

I stopped briefly and lifted my head. Her eyes were closed. A slightly shy, dreamy, blissful, deeply contented, serene smile had spread across her radiant, glistening, beautiful, soft, kind, face. She glowed.

Her pretty eyelids flickered and then she opened her eyes. They were shining, bedazzling and magnetic. "Thank you, thank you so much," she purred lovingly, before gazing hypnotically deeply into the core of my being with sweet, adorable, captivating, unconditional, spiritual love.

Again, I reminded myself what she had told me, that she was not really a dolphin, but a manifestation of my spiritual feminine ...my guiding light

She had orchestrated everything.

Tears of joy rolled down my cheeks. "Oh Nirvana, my darling, dearest, sweetest, most precious Nirvana," I sobbed.

"Nirvana, I never want you to leave my side. I love you so much it hurts. You are my world."

Nirvana looked lovingly at me. "I am touched by your concern and love," she said. "But darling Stephen, you are an animal of the land. The sea is not your environment.

"You must return to the land, where you have important work to do."

She started to tow me towards the shore. Soon, I could feel my feet dragging along the shingle and I let go of Nirvana's dorsal fin.

"I do believe this is where I came in," said Nirvana and then repeated the breathtaking somersault that had once signalled her entrance into my life.

When her grinning face surfaced again, I said: "Nirvana, I just cannot believe what has happened to me. Nor will anyone else. I guess this adventure will have to remain our secret."

"Stephen," said Nirvana, "you must learn to share. Why keep it all to yourself?"

"Don't get me wrong Nirvana," I replied. "Look, I honestly want to share my new-found knowledge with everyone. In fact, I wished I could shout it from the rooftops.

"But, honestly, I will be ridiculed if I go around telling everyone I have been speaking to a dolphin, who turned me into a spider, a tiger, a parrot, a polar bear and an elephant."

"After the courage you have shown, I would have thought the prospect of being laughed at by people with hollow, rigid minds would not bother you," said Nirvana.

"Let them laugh," she said. "After all, it is a gift to be able to make people laugh.

"It's only real men who have the courage to show their loving, tender, vulnerable, caring, giving side."

She winked, smiled and said: "and you most certainly do!

"Those who put women down, seek to suppress and deny them power and positions of authority in whatever arena in life," she said, "are spiritually unevolved and actually displaying their own weakness. Ego is in control.

"Trust me Stephen - and I know you do - from this day forth anyone who attacks you, mocks you, talks unkindly about you or betrays you, will really be harming themselves - karmically.

"For you, it should be water off a duck's - or rather a dolphin's - back.

"Don't worry about them. They must live with themselves. There are others Stephen who need to hear your tale. It will enrich their lives and will act as a sign-post on their own voyages of self-discovery."

I looked at Nirvana, intoxicated by her beauty. I knew once again I could not let her down.

"Another thing," she said. "Didn't a good friend of yours once point out to you that to reach the fruit of a tree you have to be prepared to go out on a limb?"

I gulped. "You know about that?" I exclaimed, recalling the time I had been browsing in a bookshop when a volume fell off a shelf and landed at my feet.

I bought the book, which was called OUT ON A LIMB, on impulse. As I read it, I felt I knew the authoress, as if she was a soul-mate.

The recurring theme of that book had been that to reach the fruit of a tree you had to be prepared to go out on a limb.

I was still in a state of shock when Nirvana spoke. "Your intuition told you to buy that book and when you got home that night you couldn't put it down, could you? You sat up all night, hanging on every word. Why was that?"

"Well, it just seemed to strike a chord," I replied.

"Yes, a silver cord," smiled Nirvana.

I gasped, a shudder shot down my back and I stood with my mouth wide open.

When I came round I said: "I could do with a stiff drink. My mouth is completely dry. A cool lager would not go amiss."

"Could I suggest a pint of BUDDHA-WISER," laughed Nirvana.

She sure had a great sense of humour.

I asked her: "Nirvana, just tell me please, is there anything at all about me you don't know?"

"I told you, I have been with you all your life," she said, "just hitching a ride. I am your Higher Self, your spiritual feminine, your guiding light, your God within.

"I reside in everyone, but most people prefer to keep me hidden from view, opting to live in the world of the ego self. I only appear when   someone has made strong, committed efforts to break away from their ego self.

"I have been watching you for a long time. Despite many setbacks, lows, and even bullying, you have battled your 'self'.

"Stephen, the battle is over. You have triumphed. I am your proof.

"And thank you for caring for, and always standing up for the voiceless animals no matter what. HEAVEN KNOWS, it isn't always easy!

"I can appear in all sorts of guises. For you, I chose a dolphin because I know how much you love them."

I was unshockable now.

"Okay, Nirvana," I said, "so what happens now? Do I just go up to complete strangers and tell them that I met this amazing dolphin....."

"Write it down," interjected Nirvana. "It will reach a wider, wiser audience."

"Well, I've done everything else you have suggested," I said. "So, I shall. I shall write it all down, just as it happened."

"It will be a good meditation for you," said Nirvana.

"So, I'm finally going to write a book," I stated. "I always thought I might - but this wasn't quite what I had in mind."

Nirvana interrupted: "Correction - it wasn't quite what you had in your old mind."

She added: "You will write several books, Stephen. Don't waste the knowledge that comes your way. Many people need to hear it."

"Whatever you say Nirvana," I promised.

I looked at her longingly and asked: "You will never leave me, will you?"

"Once seen, never forgotten, that's me," she promised.

"Have no fear, for fear is the obstacle to love. I could never desert you, I love you as my son. You can be sure of one thing - we'll meat* again."

(*every time I have gone to "correct" the spelling of meat, something has stopped me - could this be Nirvana giving me the title of another book?)

"One final thing sweet, sensual Stephen: Always LOVE, LOVE and LOVE. Make it your mantra."

"I love you Nirvana," I said.

"I love you, too, Stephen," she said.

We gazed at each other longingly for several seconds. Then, Nirvana winked at me, leapt high into the air, somersaulted and started to swim away from the shore and out to sea.

I started to cry. I felt I had lost my best friend in the whole world, even though she'd told me she would always be at my side.

Also, I had wanted to ask her whether I had reached my goal. Had I entered Nirvana, LAND OF LOVE?

I should have known Nirvana would have one last surprise for me.

Just before she disappeared completely from view, I saw her tail fluke rise out of the water and smash down on the surface of the sea, causing a massive wave.

The wave began to race towards the shore, overtaking and gobbling up all those ahead of it.

Finally, I watched it break a short distance away. The foamy water bubbled towards me. I watched it rush and encircle one of my feet. But this time it pushed harder and covered my other foot. I had both feet in the water now.

My tears of sorrow turned into tears of joy. I felt a thunderbolt of love surge through me. I tingled all over with love.

I looked across to the rock a short distance out to sea and there was the seagull I had seen before setting off on my journey of self-discovery. I wondered how much he had seen.

I turned round and started to walk up the beach.

After a few strides, I started to skip. I skipped and skipped for joy.

A man and his young daughter watched me.

"Look at that boy skipping, dad," said the little girl.

Her grim-looking father replied: "That's not a boy. He's a man and he should know better. He shouldn't be skipping at his age."

I stopped skipping and went over to them.

I thanked the man for showing me the error of his ways. I bent down and kissed the little girl on the forehead.

Then I carried on skipping. Skipping for joy. Just for the sheer joy of it.

I didn't care what the man thought. As I wouldn't care what he thought of my forthcoming book. But I hoped the little girl would read it one day. And that she, too, would be skipping - even when she was his age.

I arrived at my car and prepared to drive home.

I turned on the radio. Here Comes the Sun filled the airwaves.

I smiled broadly - trust Nirvana!

I turned the volume up high...and headed home.

For me, a New Age truly has arrived. Why not join me? The water's lovely and warm................!

AFTERWORD

I did not plan this book. It flowed out of me - conveying the deep, heartfelt abhorrence of cowardly cruelty to defenceless creatures I have felt since my early childhood. It was meant to be.

I feel blessed, with Nirvana's guidance, to have been able to bring it to fruition.

If its message resonated in your heart, please tell others.

Thank you!

ABOUT THE AUTHOR

Steve Charles is a former sports journalist. He now runs a pet care business. ONE FOOT IN THE WATER is his first book.